THE SCIENCE OF SONG

How and Why We Make Music

Written by

Alan Cross, Emme Cross *and* **Nicole Mortillaro**

Illustrated by

Carl Wiens

KIDS CAN PRESS

To anyone who has listened to a song and wondered, "What am I hearing?" — A.C. & E.C.

For Sara — N.M.

To my wife, Kim, an inspiration — C.W.

Published in Canada and the U.S. by Kids Can Press Ltd.
25 Dockside Drive, Toronto, ON M5A 0B5

Kids Can Press is a Corus Entertainment Inc. company

www.kidscanpress.com

The artwork in this book was rendered in Illustrator.
The text is set in Karu.

Edited by Yasemin Uçar and Kathleen Keenan
Designed by Michael Reis

Printed and bound in Shenzhen, China, in
3/2021 by C & C Offset

CM 21 0 9 8 7 6 5 4 3 2 1

Library and Archives Canada Cataloguing in Publication

Title: The science of song : how and why we make music / Alan Cross, Emme Cross, Nicole Mortillaro ; illustrated by Carl Wiens.
Names: Cross, Alan, 1962– author. | Cross, Emme, 1957– author. | Mortillaro, Nicole, 1972– author. | Wiens, Carl, illustrator.
Identifiers: Canadiana 20200372912 | ISBN 9781771387873 (hardcover)
Subjects: LCSH: Music — History and criticism — Juvenile literature. | LCSH: Music — Acoustics and physics — Juvenile literature. | LCSH: Music — Psychological aspects — Juvenile literature.
Classification: LCC ML3928 .C76 2021 | DDC j780 — dc23

Kids Can Press gratefully acknowledges that the land on which our office is located is the traditional territory of many nations, including the Mississaugas of the Credit, the Anishnabeg, the Chippewa, the Haudenosaunee and the Wendat peoples, and is now home to many diverse First Nations, Inuit and Métis peoples.

We thank the Government of Ontario, through Ontario Creates; the Ontario Arts Council; the Canada Council for the Arts; and the Government of Canada for supporting our publishing activity.

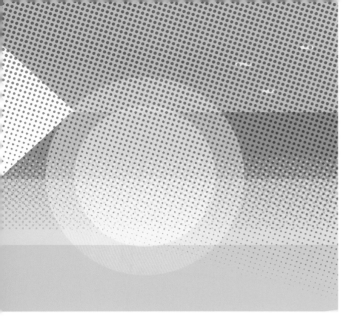

CONTENTS

THE VERY BEGINNING OF MUSIC

Have you ever wondered what makes music, well, music? How do we make it? Hear it? And why is it such a big part of our lives?

Music has been around for more than 40 000 years. Archaeologists have found evidence of music — including instruments made from animal bones and ivory — in every corner of the world. And anthropologists believe that just as animals such as birds and whales "sing" to communicate, early humans may have used music for the same purpose. Music may have also helped them create social bonds with one another.

Life has changed a lot over the past 40 000 years, but music is still very important to us. We've gone from making musical noises to communicate, to playing instruments handmade from animal bones, to inventing new forms of **artificial intelligence** that can actually create music.

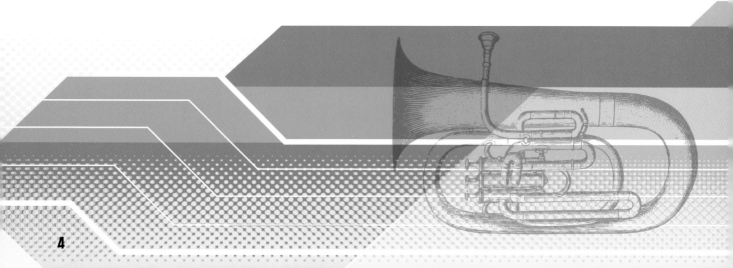

Of course, the *way* we've listened to music has changed just as much. We used to have to listen to music live — at a concert, for example. But today, we can play any song we want whenever we want, using apps and other streaming services.

In this book, you'll learn how people have transformed music over the ages, from the first time we captured **sound** to today's digital age. You'll find out how we first **recorded** music and how we kept inventing new technology to play it and make it ever more accessible. And along the way, you'll learn about the science behind such things as why your recorded voice sounds so weird, why you like the music you like and why annoying songs get stuck in your head. So put on your favorite **playlist** and let's get started ...

HEARING THINGS

To understand music, you have to understand how we hear sound. Sound is the energy objects make when they vibrate. As those vibrations travel through the air, your ears pick them up and send signals to your brain.

GETTING AN EARFUL

1. A sound enters the ear and travels through the auditory canal. Thanks to its shape, the outer ear can hear noises from every direction.

2. In the middle ear, a thin membrane called the **eardrum** moves, causing the **ossicles**, three tiny bones, to vibrate. These vibrations move into the inner ear.

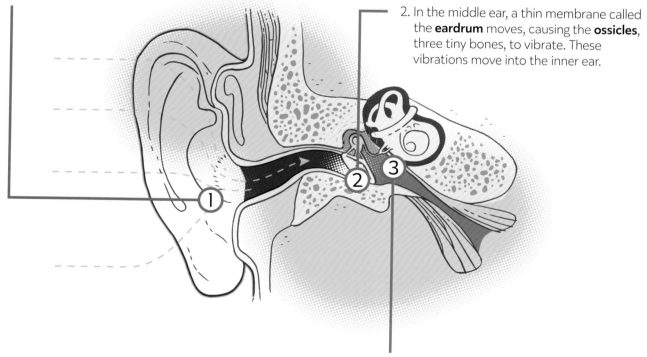

3. The vibrations hit a small, fluid-filled bone called the **cochlea**. It has about 17 000 tiny hairs that bend and create electrical signals that are sent along the **auditory nerve** to the brain. Finally, the brain translates those signals into a recognizable sound!

Have you ever heard a recording of your own voice and thought, *Do I really sound like that?!* There's a reason why you don't recognize yourself! When you talk, the vibrations of your voice enter through your ears and hit your eardrum. At the same time, they travel up through your skull and spread out inside your head. This makes the vibrations sound deeper. But when you listen to your recorded voice, you only hear the sound through your ears, not your skull, so your voice sounds higher. Your recorded voice is the one other people hear, too.

GOOD VIBRATIONS

Deaf people and those who are hard of hearing can also enjoy music. They can feel the vibrations that make sound, especially if the sound is loud and low. At some concerts, sign language interpreters stand onstage to sign lyrics to deaf concertgoers, who put the lyrics together with the vibrations to experience the music.

And being deaf doesn't mean you can't compose music. Ever heard of German composer Ludwig van Beethoven? In the early 1800s, he was starting to find fame as a composer but began to lose his hearing. By the time he was 45, he was almost completely deaf but was still composing groundbreaking pieces. One of his most famous compositions, Symphony No. 9, was composed after he had lost his hearing. Today, there are many deaf musicians, including Sean Forbes, one of the co-founders of the Deaf Professional Artist Network (D-PAN).

Playlist

Symphony No. 9 | Ludwig van Beethoven (1824)

I'm Deaf | Sean Forbes (2010)

Try | Mandy Harvey (2014)

WHAT *IS* MUSIC, ANYWAY?

If you listen to music composed by Beethoven in the 1800s and compare it with what you usually listen to (assuming that *isn't* classical music), you'll probably notice some differences. You'll hear some instruments, such as piccolos and bassoons, that you might not hear on the radio today. People may even be singing in a different style than you're used to.

All those sounds are still music. But what, exactly, *is* music?

Put simply, it's a combination of different sounds that express emotion using **melody**, **harmony** and **rhythm**. These elements work together to create a song, a symphony, or even a jingle!

Music means something different to everyone. You likely have a favorite song or even a preferred style of music, called a **genre**. Pop? Rap? Rock? Country? All different genres. Someone who prefers rap might think rock is awful, or vice versa. But they're both music, whether you like it or not.

Melody is a combination of musical notes arranged in a pattern.

Harmony is the sound two or more different notes make when played at the same time.

Rhythm is a repeating pattern of long and short notes.

THE VERY FIRST INSTRUMENTS

Can you guess what the earliest musical instrument was? The human body! Before humans made instruments from outside sources, we made music from within. The earliest humans may have used grunts and other basic sounds to communicate. Then roughly 50 000 years ago, scientists think, our vocal cords developed enough to allow speaking and singing.

Anthropologists, who study the science of human beings, aren't really sure *why* we started singing. Some scientists think early humans sang to communicate better with one another, or that mothers sang to comfort their babies. Eventually, we began making musical instruments out of wood, ivory and leftover animal bones.

Playlist

The Hurrian Hymn
Ugarit (now Syria) (1300 BCE)

Heyr himna smiður
Iceland, Kolbeinn Tumason,
adapted by Þorkell Sigurbjörnsson (1208 CE)

Sumer is icumen in
England (around 1260 CE)

In 2008, German researchers discovered a flute made from a bird bone in a cave in Germany. It's about 40 000 years old, making it the oldest recognizable musical instrument yet discovered.

MAGIC! CAPTURING SOUND

For thousands of years, humans could enjoy music only by playing the instruments they made. Whether it was a flute or a drum, when they put the instrument away, that was that — the music was gone for good.

By the 1800s, music had become a major part of people's lives. Wealthy families had pianos at home and taught their children to sing and play. Great composers (including our friend Beethoven!) wrote works that were performed in famous music halls and opera houses by skilled orchestras and singers. But only people who could afford to travel to those places could experience music. No one had invented a way to record it yet.

MAKING WAVES

The first step toward recording music happened when someone figured out that sound travels in waves. Historians think that someone was Leonardo da Vinci, an Italian inventor and artist in the 1500s. The story goes that inspiration struck when he saw a stone hit water and create ripples.

WHAT'S THAT SCREECH?

Around 1660, Italian scientist Galileo Galilei was the first to realize that how fast a sound wave moves determines that sound's **pitch** — whether it is high or low. He practiced scraping a chisel across a brass plate to make different screeching sounds. The spacing of his scrapes, meaning how far apart or close together they were, changed the screeches' pitches. And that probably made Galileo very annoying to the people around him!

SEEING SOUND

Would people ever be able to see or even capture sound waves? A few centuries later, along came Édouard-Léon Scott de Martinville, a French printer who invented a machine called the **phonautograph**. On April 9, 1860, he sang the folk song "Au clair de la lune" into a big funnel while turning a cylinder covered in greasy soot. The vibrations of his voice traveled down the funnel to a pointy piece of metal. The metal vibrated in time with his voice, scratching zigs and zags into the soot on the cylinder. It was the first time anyone had "seen" sound waves. But there was no way to play them back — yet.

In 2008, scientists in Berkeley, California, turned Scott de Martinville's scratches into actual sound. It may be the earliest recognizable recording of the human voice.

Playlist

Swing Low, Sweet Chariot | Wallace Willis (1800s)

Row, Row, Row Your Boat | original composer unknown (around 1840)

Chopsticks | Euphemia Allen (1877)

WRITING WITH SOUND

The curious Scott de Martinville was able to capture, but not play back, sound. Then, in 1877, inventor Thomas Edison unveiled an invention called the **phonograph** (a Greek word meaning "sound writing"). It could record sound *and* play it back — here's how.

1. A cylinder covered in tinfoil was rotated by a hand crank 120 times a minute.

2. Meanwhile, a cone-shaped horn funneled sound down to a tiny tube, concentrating the sound waves into a small space.

3. The sound waves bounced into a thin piece of cloth called a **membrane**.

4. An attached needle called a **stylus** vibrated in exact time with the sound, digging a groove into the tinfoil. The groove was where the sound was captured.

5. To listen to the recording, the stylus was moved back to the beginning of the groove and the cylinder cranked once again. As the stylus traced the path of the groove, it vibrated the **diaphragm**, producing sound that was funneled out the horn.

Phonographs had no volume controls. So listeners who wanted to lower the volume jammed a fabric ball called a sock into the horn to muffle the sound. That's the origin of the phrase "Stick a sock in it!"

Though early recordings of Black artists are rare, the first Black singer to make a record may have been George W. Johnson, a New York City street performer, in 1890. Johnson went on to become the first bestselling Black recording artist.

MUSIC FOR ALL

Tinfoil was easily damaged, produced crackly sounds and wore out after a couple of plays. So Edison tried sturdier cylinders covered in wax. These sounded better and could be played about 100 times. But the phonograph wasn't perfect. It was hard to capture sound with a horn, so singers had to sing very close to it, especially if it was a quiet song. Loud instruments such as trumpets had to be stationed farther back so they didn't overpower the others.

Even so, the phonograph changed music forever. People no longer had to travel to attend performances. Now, families who could afford a phonograph enjoyed music in their own homes. They could even record sound and play it back themselves.

Playlist

By the Light of the Silvery Moon
Billy Murray and the Haydn Quartet (1910)

Over There
George M. Cohan (1917)

Trouble in Mind
Bertha "Chippie" Hill, Richard M. Jones and Louis Armstrong (1926)

THE RISE OF RADIO

In 1901, Italian engineer Guglielmo Marconi sent the first transatlantic radio signal (an *S* in Morse code) from Cornwall, England, to Newfoundland, Canada. But Canadian inventor Reginald Aubrey Fessenden was convinced that radio could transmit more than just simple Morse code, which used dots and dashes to spell out messages. In 1906, Fessenden became the first person to send the human voice over a radio signal.

By the late 1920s, radio was being used all over the world for communication, news and music, too. This was a whole new way of listening to music — someone choosing songs *for* you. It was almost like a concert, where you didn't know what wonderful tune you'd hear next.

GLUED TO THE RADIO

Soon, radio stations started airing weekly series such as *Amos 'n' Andy*, *The Green Hornet* and *The Tenth Man*. With dialogue, music and sound effects, a radio series was like a play you heard instead of watched (almost like a podcast!).

Radio united people as families gathered to listen together. To make listening even more enjoyable, manufacturers introduced radios set in fancy wood cabinets that looked like furniture. These systems worked using **vacuum tubes** — big, delicate bulbs of glass and wire that consumed electricity and gave off a lot of heat. Like light bulbs, they often burned out, causing the radio to go dead. There was still room for improvement.

ALIENS INVADE!

Would you believe a radio broadcast about aliens invading Earth? In 1938, one such broadcast caused panic in New York City. American actor and director Orson Welles read a radio play based on H. G. Wells's science fiction novel *The War of the Worlds*. Some listeners thought they were hearing a terrifying true account of aliens invading Earth. Eventually, Welles had to explain that it was just a radio program.

The Daily
RADIO PLAY TERRIFIES NATION
Mars Invasion Thought Real

The first headphones were invented in the 1890s. Some were huge, weighing up to 3 kg (6.6 lbs.), a little heavier than a brick. Imagine wearing those! Over the years, people tried to improve the design, including French engineer Ernest Mercadier and American inventor Nathaniel Baldwin, who created a pair for the U.S. Navy in 1910. In the late 1950s, companies started selling headphones designed for listening to music.

Playlist

Nobody Knows You When You're Down and Out
Bessie Smith (1929)

Pennies from Heaven
Bing Crosby (1936)

Over the Rainbow
Judy Garland (1939)

THE RECORD TAKES SHAPE

While people were listening to phonographs, Emile Berliner, a German-born American inventor, thought there must be a better way to capture sound than carving grooves on wax cylinders. The recordings quickly wore out and couldn't be easily mass produced. Popular singers had to record their songs thousands of times!

In 1887, Berliner had a flash of inspiration: why not carve those grooves as a spiral on a flat rotating disc? He created a device called the **gramophone** to play the new discs. Each side of a disc held three to four minutes of music.

Berliner's discs were made of shellac, a material that came from bug goo! The female lac bug, found in southeast Asia, produces resin, a substance that was used to make shellac.

ON THE RECORD

In 1948, CBS, the company that owned Columbia Records, started using a more durable type of plastic called **polyvinyl chloride (PVC)** on their records. Success! The sound hissed and crackled less, and you could place the grooves closer together to fit more music on the record.

There were two common record sizes: the **LP**, or "long-playing" record, and the **45**. The LP was also called an **album**, the term we still use today to describe a collection of songs that are connected by mood or style and recorded together. In the 1960s, popular artists such as Bob Dylan, the Beatles and the Beach Boys began to focus on creating albums instead of releasing songs one at a time.

LP
30.5 cm (12 in.) diameter
rotated at 33 $\frac{1}{3}$ revolutions per minute (RPM)
22 minutes of music per side

45
17.9 cm (7 in.) diameter
rotated at 45 RPM
6–7 minutes of music per side

Playlist

Boogie Woogie Bugle Boy
The Andrews Sisters (1941)

Maybellene
Chuck Berry (1955)

Love Me Do
The Beatles (1962)

The first records were produced in **mono**, meaning that to listeners, all the music seemed to come from a single direction. In the real world, though, we hear sounds coming from all directions. By 1958, engineers had figured out how to use two microphones to record in **stereo**, meaning with sounds coming from two different directions. By balancing what sounds went through each speaker, sound engineers could create a realistic recording. Music has been recorded that way ever since!

IT'S ALL IN YOUR HEAD

Think about how music is used in horror movies, such as John Williams's score for *Jaws*. Just as someone gets in the water, the music changes to a creepy theme that puts you on the edge of your seat, waiting … Will the shark attack?

Music can have a strong effect on you. Scientists are still trying to understand exactly what happens to your brain when you listen to music, but they do know that a lot happens at once. Sound travels from your ears to the **auditory cortex**, the part of your brain that processes sound. But it doesn't stop there. Most of your brain is involved in listening to music, including the parts that process speech, vision and emotional responses. Scientists even think there are some brain cells, called **neurons**, that are meant specifically for processing music.

MUSICAL MEMORIES

Music is so powerful that it may even help patients with brain disorders. Scientists think that people who have Alzheimer's, a disease that affects the brain's ability to think and remember, are still able to recognize their favorite music. In one 2018 study, researchers at the University of Toronto found that listening to music helped some Alzheimer's patients recall memories associated with that music.

In a 1999 study, psychologists Andrea Halpern and Robert J. Zatorre scanned people's brains while they were imagining listening to a piece of music. Just imagining the music lit up many parts of the brain that had been activated when people were actually listening.

WORMS IN YOUR BRAIN

Your brain is also responsible for earworms — those pesky songs you can't get out of your head. British music psychologist Victoria Williamson conducted a study to find out what causes them. She discovered that an "earworm" song was usually both catchy (attention-grabbing) and easy to remember. Earworms are like musical memories: which ones we experience depend on what music is meaningful to us. In another study, British researcher Kelly Jakubowski found that songs with a faster pace and unusual breaks and repetitions seem more likely to get stuck in our heads.

Most earworms are about eight seconds' worth of music. Want to get rid of them? Scientists suggest listening to the entire song or trying to distract yourself. (Good luck!)

Playlist

Jingle Bells | James Lord Pierpont (1857)

We Will Rock You | Queen (1977)

Bad Romance | Lady Gaga (2009)

LISTENING ON THE GO

Today, it's normal to take music with us everywhere. But that didn't start until 1947, when Bell Labs unveiled a device called the **transistor** that allowed electronics to be made smaller and more energy efficient. The first device made with the new technology was a hearing aid. The second was a transistor radio, the Regency TR-1. It cost $49.95 (almost $500 today). Other companies began to make their own versions, and by the 1960s prices had dropped and everyone wanted one.

Transistor radios were lighter, smaller and portable because they were powered by batteries. They were especially popular with teenagers, who could now take their music wherever they went.

MAGNETIC MUSIC

Around the time records were first developed, engineers in the United States and Denmark had experimented with using tape and wire to store sound. But wire could get twisted and become unusable. In the 1920s, German scientist Fritz Pfleumer invented "sounding paper," a type of paper coated with magnetic particles. When it kept tearing, he switched to plastic tape similar to photographic film.

CASSETTES DO IT ALL

Sounding paper didn't catch on, but by the 1960s, the Dutch company Philips had introduced the **cassette**. It was a teeny tiny tape system inside a plastic case about the size of a deck of cards. Much easier to take on the go! You could record on it, fast-forward and rewind, too. Each cassette held up to 60 minutes of music per side (and cassettes that could hold even more were soon invented).

Cassettes were much easier to make than records. In the 1970s and '80s, hip-hop artist Grandmaster Flash recorded special tapes for some fans, often including their names in his raps.

SPOOLING OUT

So how does a cassette work? It's not that different from how Pfleumer first imagined it. Tiny metal particles are glued to a thin, narrow length of tape. That tape is put on a spool. When music is being recorded, the tape rolls from the right spool to the left, passing over a recording head that turns an electrical signal into magnetized patterns. Those patterns are captured on the tape — they're the sounds being recorded.

When music is played, the tape is run over a playback head. It picks up the patterns and turns them back into electrical signals and then sounds that we can hear.

Playlist
Return to Sender | Elvis Presley (1962)
Respect | Aretha Franklin (1967)
(Sittin' on) The Dock of the Bay | Otis Redding (1968)

THE "MAN" WHO CHANGED MUSIC FOREVER

By the end of the 1970s, the most convenient, portable and versatile recorded music format was the cassette. But could it be made even *more* convenient? On July 1, 1979, one of the most revolutionary music devices in the history of humankind was introduced: the Sony Walkman. It was a cassette player the size of a paperback book with amazingly lightweight headphones attached. It cost $150 (over $500 today).

PARTY OF ONE

The original Walkman had two headphone jacks so that two people could listen at once. Sony engineers couldn't believe that anyone would want to walk around listening alone, isolated from everything around them. Until then, music had been mostly a communal experience. Whether you were listening in a concert hall, to the radio at home, or to a record player at a party, everyone around you was able to hear what you heard. Since the invention of the Walkman, though, private listening has become normal. How many people have you seen wearing headphones or earbuds just today?

MIXING IT UP

The idea of **mixtapes**, or tapes that include a mix of songs by different artists, took off with the Walkman. People bought blank cassettes by the dozens, creating their own mixes that they could take with them everywhere and trade with friends. Today, we do a version of the same thing — but we call them "playlists."

Making mixtapes wasn't as easy as putting together a playlist with just a few clicks. Back then, one way was to record songs from the radio, which meant waiting for a radio station to play the right song. Or you could use a kind of portable music player called a double-cassette boombox to copy songs from one tape to another.

While we may love to listen alone with headphones, a 2017 study conducted by Australian researchers Melissa Weinberg and Dawn Joseph suggests that going to concerts and singing and dancing with others actually improves both our mental health and our general well-being.

Playlist

Jolene | Dolly Parton (1973)

How Deep Is Your Love | The Bee Gees (1977)

I Will Survive | Gloria Gaynor (1979)

IDEAS THAT BOMBED

Believe it or not, not all new ideas are good. Now that you know about some of the most successful inventions in music history, let's look at some ideas that, well, flopped. Big time.

THE KA-THUNK THAT STUNK

After World War II ended in 1945, many families moved away from big cities into the suburbs. While driving the long distances to get to work, people wanted to listen to their own music. In 1966, the car company Ford introduced an even smaller version of the cassette, called the **8-track**, in its new cars. The 8-track had a long, continuous loop of tape inside a plastic case called a cartridge. The tape had four "programs," kind of like the sides of a record. Each program was divided into two channels, resulting in eight (or 4 x 2) tracks.

One 8-track could hold up to 80 minutes of music. But the tape ran in only one direction, so you had to fast-forward to find the song you wanted to hear. Sometimes there were long silences or a jarring ka-THUNK sound right in the middle of a song, as the player switched to the next program. Thanks to the popularity of the cassette, the 8-track never quite caught on, and production stopped in 1982.

SMALLER ISN'T ALWAYS BETTER

Another idea that bombed was the microcassette. It was about one-fourth the size of a standard cassette and held 30 minutes of audio per side. Some people thought this smaller version might be more convenient and portable — but it wasn't. Microcassettes were recorded and played at a slower speed than regular cassettes, which produced more background noise and a lower sound quality. Plus they were so small they were easy to lose!

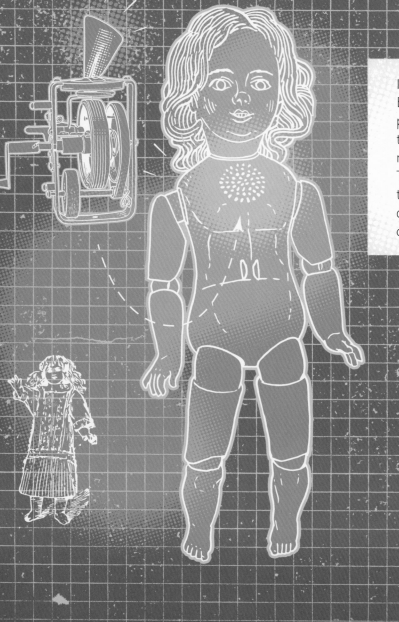

It isn't only modern ideas that bomb. Back in 1877, just after he invented the phonograph, Edison created a tiny version that could fit inside a doll and play a nursery rhyme. Unfortunately, the Edison Talking Doll was a failure. Not only did the wax records inside the dolls wear out quickly, the sound quality was poor and children found them a bit creepy.

Playlist

Love to Love You Baby
Donna Summer (1975)

Tainted Love
Soft Cell (1981)

Smalltown Boy
Bronski Beat (1984)

VIDEO STARS

On December 2, 1983, people all over the United States and Canada gathered around their television sets. They weren't watching the premiere of a TV show or a big news event. Instead, they were eagerly waiting for a new music video on the channel Music Television (MTV): Michael Jackson's "Thriller."

At the time, music videos often showed the band or artist singing, dancing or playing a concert. "Thriller," though, was more like a mini movie. It was directed by respected film director John Landis and narrated by horror movie star Vincent Price. "Thriller" was a new kind of music video, but the idea of pairing music with images had been around for almost a century.

1894: Music publishers Edward B. Marks and Joe Stern hire musicians to play their song "The Little Lost Child" while images are projected on a screen. "Illustrated songs" become very popular at theaters.

1895: Inventor William Dickson makes a 17-second sound film. He plays a violin while two men dance.

1929: A 16-minute film shows singer Bessie Smith and two actors portraying the events of her song "St. Louis Blues" while the song plays.

1940: Three-minute musical videos called soundies, played in a coin-operated jukebox, become popular in restaurants and nightclubs.

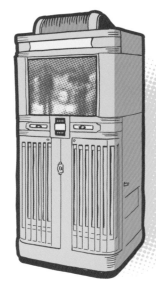

1964: The Beatles star in *A Hard Day's Night*, a comedy film based on their lives and featuring their songs.

1965: In a film clip for his song "Subterranean Homesick Blues," Bob Dylan holds up cue cards with the lyrics on them.

1975: British rock band Queen perform their new single "Bohemian Rhapsody" in a music video. The video makes the song a hit, and other artists begin to create music videos to promote new music.

1981: MTV, an all-music TV channel, takes to the airwaves on August 1 and plays its very first music video, "Video Killed the Radio Star" by The Buggles.

1983: Michael Jackson's "Thriller" debuts on MTV. Nearly 14 minutes long, it cost almost $1 million (about $3 million today) to make.

1984: In Canada, TV channel MuchMusic debuts with "Snappy Songs" by Eubie Blake, a short film from the 1920s.

1993–1997: MTV opens new channels in countries around the world, including China and India.

2005: YouTube launches, making it easier than ever for artists to promote their music using videos.

2016: Beyoncé releases *Lemonade*, a visual album. In addition to 12 songs, *Lemonade* includes a 65-minute film.

Playlist

What's Love Got to Do with It? | Tina Turner (1981)

Every Breath You Take | The Police (1983)

Vogue | Madonna (1990)

BYE, VINYL!

After the invention of cassettes, people listened to them on the go and still played records at home. But another big musical change was coming: a move from analog to digital technology.

Scientists describe analog sound as "continuous sound waves that change in frequency and volume." Those changes are captured during recording, so analog recording represents the sounds we hear in real life. Digital recording is different — it breaks down the sound into data in a process called digitizing sound. Your favorite song becomes a string of zeros and ones called binary code. A digital recording can sometimes sound cleaner than an analog recording. The sound is pure and crisp with no crackling or interference. The compact disc (CD) was developed to play digitized sound.

HOW A CD WORKS

1. A CD stores music by converting an analog signal into binary code.
2. The code is stored in a pattern of microscopic pits on a disc.
3. The disc is read with a laser. The laser converts information stored in the pits back into an electrical signal that is then sent to an amplifier and speakers.

SMOOTH SOUND

Unlike records and cassettes, CDs had no crackling, popping or annoying background hiss. Plus CD players made it easy to skip songs: you just pushed a button to get to the next track. (Compare that to having to fast-forward a cassette tape!) In fact, researchers at the Ohio State University think that people's musical attention spans started to shorten when it became so easy to skip songs.

At first, record labels and stores weren't fond of the CD. Record labels were disturbed by how easy it was to copy the music. Producers had to make both vinyl *and* CDs, and stores had to stock both, plus cassettes. Eventually, though, CDs won. By 1988, sales of CDs were more than double the sales of LPs in the United States, and by 1992, CD sales passed cassette sales.

Playlist

Nothing Compares 2 U
Sinéad O'Connor (1990)

The Sign
Ace of Base (1993)

Macarena (Bayside Boys Mix)
Los del Río (1996)

In a 2017 study, Canadian musicologist Hubert Léveillé Gauvin found that musical introductions in songs have become four times shorter than they were in 1986. Thanks to our shorter attention spans, songs need to grab us fast or they get skipped.

WHY YOU LIKE WHAT YOU LIKE

Ever wondered why you like the music you do? Scientists wonder that, too. In 2016, American neuroscientists and anthropologists traveled to Bolivia to meet the Tsimané, an Indigenous group that hadn't been exposed to much Western music. Scientists played them music that, in Western culture, was considered to be **consonant**, or pleasant and harmonious, and music that was **dissonant**, or clashing and not harmonious.

The Tsimané rated both types of music the same and didn't prefer one over the other. This study helped scientists realize that our general musical preferences may be cultural, meaning we learn them as we grow up. They aren't something we're born with.

(DON'T) CHANGE YOUR TUNE

Individual people also have favorite musical genres. Why does listening to Selena Gomez make one person smile and another one cringe? Your individual musical preference may depend on your environment and personality. In a 2016 study, British and Finnish researchers discovered that people who are empathetic (care a lot about the feelings of others) liked music that was low energy and conveyed sad emotions. People who are systematic (prefer patterns and rules) liked intense music, such as hard rock and metal. And people who said they were both empathetic and systematic? They liked a little of both.

OUR MUSIC, OUR SELVES

Our taste in music sometimes changes. The musicians you listen to now likely won't be the ones you listen to in your 40s (though they'll always have a special place in your heart!). Some researchers suspect our taste changes as we age. When we're younger, we prefer intense music that gives us strong feelings and helps us develop a sense of self. In early adulthood, we like current, popular music. Finally, as we age, we begin to appreciate more complex music, such as classical. Do you think your taste in music will change?

Oddly, sometimes listening to your favorite sad music makes you feel better. Blame your brain! In a 2011 study, American professor David Huron found that when you listen to sorrowful tunes, your brain releases the chemical prolactin, which may have a soothing effect. And listening to music you love, sad or happy, releases another chemical, dopamine, that makes you feel good.

Playlist

The Wheels on the Bus
Verna Hills (1939)

I'm a Little Teapot
George Harold Sanders and
Clarence Z. Kelley (1939)

Baby Shark
Pinkfong (2015)

MUSIC IN THE DIGITAL AGE

Believe it or not, you can thank hockey for MP3s, the digital musical format that changed everything — again! In 1991, the Fraunhofer Institute, a German research institute, was looking for a way to send large audio files over phone lines. It's challenging to compress, or shrink, music files so they're small enough to send without losing any of the sound quality. It was especially difficult to compress audio from a hockey game, thanks to sounds such as those made by skates slashing the ice, pucks booming off boards and crowds cheering. Once engineers had normal-sounding compressed hockey audio, they knew they were on to something: the MP3.

MP3 technology is based on the principles of **psychoacoustics**, the scientific study of how humans hear sounds. We hear layers and layers of sound all at once, but we don't *fully* hear or recognize all those sounds at once. MP3s are created using **algorithms**, or mathematical instructions, that strip out the hidden layers of sound. The algorithms convert audio into an MP3 and make the file smaller.

ONE SONG AT A TIME

Many new devices were invented to play MP3s, but the most popular was Apple's iPod, which arrived in 2001 along with the iTunes Music Store. Not only could you buy digital versions of songs legally, you could carry them all around in your pocket. Within five years, Apple had sold a billion songs. Today, that number is in the tens of billions.

After 2001, CD sales fell faster and faster. People no longer had to buy entire albums to get one or two favorite songs. Plus buying (or stealing!) music online was easier and cheaper. Record stores were forced to close, and musicians had to find ways of replacing the money they lost from CD sales. For years, the record industry struggled to adapt.

MP3s quickly became very popular. Some music fans began turning songs on CDs into MP3s and trading them online (also known as **piracy**). And free file-sharing companies such as Napster made that very easy. Founded in 1999, Napster had more than 80 million registered users at one point. Finally, record companies began to sue for copyright infringement.

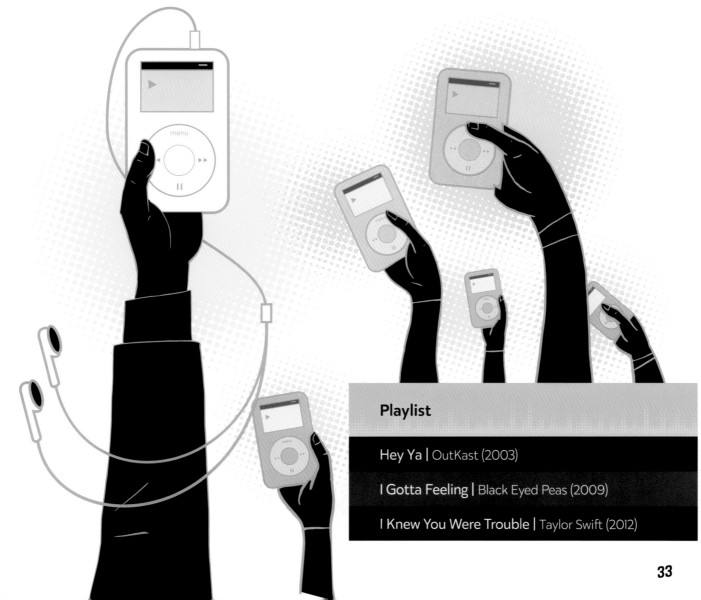

Playlist

Hey Ya | OutKast (2003)

I Gotta Feeling | Black Eyed Peas (2009)

I Knew You Were Trouble | Taylor Swift (2012)

BEYOND LISTENING

Music is all around us — you can't escape it! It's playing in shopping malls, supermarkets and airports, on the phone when you're on hold and even in elevators. Sometimes that music is just there to fill up silence, but sometimes it's used to influence you. The type of music playing in a mall or supermarket isn't random but carefully selected. You might think most of the time you're not even listening to it. But even if your conscious mind isn't paying attention ... your unconscious mind is!

THE POWER OF MUSIC

In a 1982 study, American marketing professor Ronald E. Milliman found that loud music with a faster beat makes people shop faster. That's not good for stores because it's likely that the longer you shop, the more you'll buy. Another study in 2011, led by German researcher Klemens Michael Knöferle, suggested that when a supermarket played slow, sad music, sales were 12 percent higher.

And have you ever noticed that you hear Christmas music earlier and earlier each year? That's because studies have found that playing Christmas music subconsciously influences shoppers to buy more Christmas-related goods. Sneaky! So next time you hear slow, sad Christmas music, resist the urge to buy everything you see.

How do you get rid of teenagers? By playing some Beethoven or Mozart, apparently. Some public places, such as train stations and some stores, play classical music in an effort to keep young people from loitering.

SHOP TILL YOU DROP

In 2000, American researchers Richard Yalch and Eric Spangenberg found that music affects how we think about time when we're shopping. They created a pretend shop and played music that was both familiar and unfamiliar to study participants. When people shopped with no time limit and familiar music playing, they spent almost 8 percent less time shopping than when they listened to unfamiliar music. When they listened to unfamiliar music, they felt time passed more quickly. Yalch and Spangenberg concluded that when the customers were paying attention to music they knew, time seemed to pass more slowly. This made them rush through the store.

Playlist

Lost in the Supermarket | The Clash (1979)

Shopping | The Jam (1982)

I Am a Grocery Bag | They Might Be Giants (2001)

IN THE PALM OF YOUR HAND

Consider what you've read about how people used to listen to music 10, 50 or 100 years ago. Music was once something people could only hear live and has become digital codes saved in pocket-sized devices. You can now access just about any song ever recorded, as long as you have an internet connection.

THE BIRTH OF STREAMING

Why download anything if the internet has it all? That's the idea behind streaming music. A giant record store might have 100 000 albums in stock. But streaming music companies have massive collections of songs — tens of millions of digital music files. Streaming allows you to access all those songs from wherever you are, often for a monthly fee.

The very first company to offer legal streaming was Rhapsody in 2001. Since then, we've seen Spotify, Apple Music, Last.Fm, Beats Music, Google Play Music, Tidal, Xbox Music and many, many others. Even Napster is now a legal streaming service. Competition is very fierce, and many streaming companies (such as 8tracks and Rdio) don't survive beyond a few years. But each year, the idea of "renting" music grows in popularity. Spotify went from 18 million subscribers in 2015 to 115 million in 2019.

YouTube is one way many artists can launch entire careers. Ever heard of Justin Bieber? Growing up, he lived in Stratford, a small town in southwestern Ontario, Canada. After he won a local talent show, his family posted videos of him singing on the newly launched YouTube. In 2008, a big music executive came across one of these home videos. Intrigued, he tracked Bieber down and convinced him to sign with the record label — and the rest is history.

VINYL MAKES A COMEBACK

After hitting an all-time low in 2007, vinyl sales rebounded as people rediscovered this old-fashioned way of collecting and listening to music. In 2020, vinyl outsold CDs for the first time since the 1980s. Why? Maybe some people like to hold their music in their hands. Maybe they don't like the digital sound and prefer the richer, less perfect sound quality of vinyl. Or maybe they're just into collecting. In this case, everything old is new again!

Playlist

Hello | Adele (2015)

4:44 | Jay-Z (2017)

you should see me in a crown
Billie Eilish (2019)

ARTIFICIAL MUSIC

You don't need to be Beethoven or Beyoncé to make music — anyone can. You can sit down at a piano and compose a song. You can whistle a melody you made up or clap your hands to create a rhythm. But can any*thing* make music?

Computer systems called artificial intelligence (AI), which perform human-like tasks and have the ability to learn, have become more and more common. Recently, scientists have started experimenting with creative AI that can make art and compose music.

In 2005, IBM began developing a computer system nicknamed Watson to play the quiz game *Jeopardy!* That eventually led to Watson Beat, which helps artists create original music compositions. After being fed data, such as the sounds of different instruments, Watson Beat creates different melodies, pitches and rhythms. Grammy Award–winning producer and composer Alex da Kid used Watson Beat to come up with the hit song "Not Easy."

Another company, Aiva Technologies, trained its computer with classical music, including works by Beethoven, Mozart, Bach and more. The AIVA (artificial intelligence virtual artist) composer has been used to create movie and video game soundtracks.

How does a computer learn? The process is called deep learning. Large amounts of data are programmed into artificial intelligence systems, allowing them to learn from experience. An algorithm is then programmed into the computer. As more and more information is added, the AI can improve its original algorithm.

MUSIC BY THE NUMBERS

You don't even need to play an instrument to create music. Companies like Amper Music and Jukedeck turn ordinary people into composers. Choose a genre and from there, you can pick a mood, tempo and more to create an original piece of music developed by AI. With all this new technology comes fear that composers and musicians may be out of jobs. While the way we do things may change, it's unlikely that there will be no more human composers and musicians. AI may be able to create music, but humans are ultimately in charge.

Google's musical AI, NSynth, combines the sounds of different instruments, such as guitar and piano, into one new sound. It's an open-source project, meaning anyone can use it for free.

Playlist

Symphonic Fantasy for Orchestra in A Minor | Op. 21: Genesis, Aiva (2016)

Daddy's Car | Sony CSL and Benoît Carré (2016)

Break Free | Amper and Taryn Southern (2017)

WHAT'S NEXT

At the 2012 Coachella Valley Music and Arts Festival in Indio, California, the crowd was shocked to see Tupac Shakur take to the stage. Why were they so surprised? Tupac died in 1996! The dead rapper was "brought to life" using technology similar to **holograms**. And it looked *real*.

While the technology behind this "trick" dates back to the 1860s, it isn't easy to create. It took six months to build Tupac's "back-from-the-dead" performance — based on his past performances — and it cost almost half a million dollars. The technology is constantly being refined to make these ghostly performances look ever more realistic. Concerts featuring holograms could soon become more common.

The idea of creating a two-dimensional, almost ghost-like apparition was first tried out in the 1860s by engineer Henry Dircks and scientist John Henry Pepper. An actor stayed offstage in a hidden room while Dircks and Pepper used glass and light to project his image. When light hit the glass in a certain way, a ghostly image of the actor — really just his reflection in the glass — appeared onstage.

FEEL THE BEAT

Some people believe that music will eventually be delivered through **biometrics**. We'll all have implants that will sense our mood or heartbeat and automatically play the perfect music for the occasion, right through our bodies. For example, some people with hearing loss now use small electronic devices called cochlear implants to hear sounds. Similar implant technology could allow anyone to listen to music without even using headphones.

Don't count it out. After all, in a 2003 interview, Apple founder Steve Jobs said he didn't believe people would pay for a subscription to download or stream music. "The subscription model of buying music is bankrupt," he said. How wrong he was.

Imagine telling Edison about artificial intelligence and the iPhone. Back in 1877, no one could have predicted what music would look like today. What we now take for granted would seem like magic to someone born just two centuries ago. And more magic is coming. Two hundred years from today, how people listen to music will have changed in ways we can't even imagine.

Playlist

The Lover's Ghost
Ralph Vaughan Williams (1913)

(Ghost) Riders in the Sky
Johnny Cash (1979)

Dead Souls
Nine Inch Nails (1994)

TIMELINE

You've read all about some of the most important inventions in music. But music has been around for a long time — over 40 000 years, to be exact — and a lot has happened since early humans made the first animal-bone flute. Here's a look at some other important moments in musical history.

50 000 years ago: human vocal cords develop enough for speaking and singing

40 000 years ago: early humans use their own bodies and instruments made of animal bone to make music

around 1000: composers start to create the written system of music still used today

1098: birth of Hildegard of Bingen, one of the first known female composers

up to 1400: early music is mostly sung and often associated with religious celebrations

1400: beginning of the Renaissance Period

early 1500s: invention of the violin, viola and cello

1598: the first opera, *Dafne* by Jacopo Peri and Jacopo Corsi, is performed in Italy

1600: beginning of the Baroque Period

around 1600: stringed instruments called Baroque guitars, based on earlier instruments the lute and the oud, become popular

1660: Galileo Galilei practices making sound waves on a brass plate

around 1700: invention of the piano

1750: beginning of the Classical Period

1770: birth of Ludwig van Beethoven, who continued composing music after he lost his hearing

1792: birth of Francis "Frank" Johnson, the first Black composer to give public concerts

1820: beginning of the Romantic Period

1860: Édouard-Léon Scott de Martinville invents the phonautograph

1870s: the musical style of blues is developed by Black musicians and composers in the southern United States

1877: Thomas Edison invents the phonograph

1885: birth of Gid Tanner, who becomes one of the first popular country music artists

1887: Emile Berliner invents the gramophone

1890s: first headphones invented

1900: beginning of the Modernist Period

1901: Guglielmo Marconi sends the first transatlantic radio signal

1915: birth of gospel musician Sister Rosetta Tharpe, who would later be known as the "godmother of rock and roll" thanks to her influential electric guitar technique

1920s: radio grows in popularity and spreads around the world

1920s: Fritz Pfleumer invents sounding paper

1920s: Chinese Americans pay to bring Cantonese opera troupes to the United States to perform

1922: birth of George Walker, the first Black American composer to win a Pulitzer Prize for music

1931: George Beauchamp and Adolph Rickenbacker receive a patent to make the first electric guitars

1947: invention of the transistor

1948: Columbia Records starts using plastic records

1951: "Rocket 88," one of the first rock and roll songs, is recorded by Jackie Brenston and the Delta Cats

1960s: Philips introduces the cassette

1970s: in the United Kingdom, British Punjabi musicians popularize bhangra, a musical style based on Punjabi folk music and influenced by rock

1975: birth of Tanya Tagaq, an Inuit musician who performs traditional throat singing in her music

1979: Sony sells the first Walkman

1979: "Rapper's Delight" by the Sugarhill Gang becomes one of the first hit rap songs in North America

1981: MTV plays its first music video

1982: the first compact disc (CD) is produced

1983: singer-songwriter Buffy Sainte-Marie becomes the first Indigenous person to win the Academy Award for Best Original Song for the song "Up Where We Belong"

1991: the Fraunhofer Institute creates the MP3

2001: Apple introduces the iPod, a portable device for playing digital music

2001: the first legal music streaming site, Rhapsody, opens

2012: a hologram of Tupac Shakur performs at the Coachella Festival

2018: video-sharing app TikTok, which many aspiring artists use to upload short music videos, becomes the most-downloaded app in the United States

2019: Spotify hits 115 million subscribers

2020: during the COVID-19 global pandemic, artists are forced to cancel in-person concerts. Musicians of all genres turn to streaming, airing concerts that people around the world can watch online.

GLOSSARY

album: a group of songs recorded and released as a collection under one title

algorithm: a set of rules or mathematical instructions that solve a problem or complete a task

artificial intelligence (AI): computer systems that perform human-like tasks and have the ability to learn

auditory cortex: the area of the brain that processes sound

auditory nerve: the nerve in the ear that carries electrical signals from the cochlea to the brain

biometrics: the use of unique physical characteristics, such as a fingerprint or voice, often to verify identity

cassette: a plastic case that contains a spool of magnetic tape, used for recording or playing back sound

cochlea: a small, fluid-filled bone in the inner ear that turns vibrations into sound signals to send to the brain

consonant: pleasant and harmonious

diaphragm: a flat, flexible membrane in a traditional phonograph or gramophone that converts vibration to sound

dissonant: clashing and unpleasant

eardrum: an air-filled flap of skin in the middle ear that vibrates when sound hits it

8-track: a plastic case containing magnetic tape divided into four different programs, used for recording or playing back sound

45: a vinyl record, seven inches in diameter, designed to spin 45 times a minute and hold six or seven minutes of music per side

genre: a category or style of music

gramophone: a device invented by Emile Berliner that uses a flat spinning disc to record or play sound

harmony: the pleasing sound two or more different notes make when played at the same time

hologram: a 3D image produced using reflected light

long-playing record (LP): a vinyl record designed to spin 33 $\frac{1}{3}$ times a minute and hold up to 22 minutes of music per side

melody: a combination of musical notes arranged in a pattern

membrane: in a phonograph, a thin piece of cloth or other material that vibrates in time with sound

mixtape: a tape made up of different songs by various artists, often recorded from different sources

mono: a way of recording music in which all sound comes from a single path or direction

neurons: cells in the brain that carry electrical signals

ossicles: three tiny bones in the middle ear that vibrate when sound hits them

phonautograph: a device that captured sound waves on a piece of paper or sheet of glass covered in soot

phonograph: a device invented by Thomas Edison that uses a spinning cylinder to record or play sound, eventually replaced by the gramophone

piracy: the illegal copying and distribution of music one does not own the copyright to

pitch: the measure of the vibration of a musical note, indicating how high or low a sound is

playlist: a list of different songs by various artists, organized for streaming or playing on the radio

polyvinyl chloride (PVC): a tough, resistant type of plastic used to make pipes, records and many other products

psychoacoustics: the scientific study of how humans hear sounds

record (verb): to capture soundwaves so that they can be played again and reproduced

rhythm: a repeating pattern of long and short notes or beats

sound: the energy objects make when they vibrate

stereo: a way of recording music in which sound comes from multiple paths or directions

stylus: on a phonograph, a needle that vibrates in time to sound and digs a groove across a piece of tinfoil to record the sound

transistor: a device used in electronics to switch or amplify an electronic current

vacuum tubes: electronic devices made of big, delicate bulbs of glass and wire that transmit electronic signals

AUTHORS' NOTE

The roots of this book go back to a phone call about a new museum exhibit called *The Science of Rock*, which would tour science centres around the continent. Would we be willing to help contribute by researching and writing for it? Absolutely! So we did. The exhibit proved to be very popular wherever it was staged.

The exhibit also explained how science, technology and engineering advances gave us the music we love to listen to today — and the methods we use to listen to it. Put that together with the history of music and you get this book.

We hope that this book will be a jumping-off point for some new adventures in music. There are many more inventors and artists worth exploring. There's the entire history of how ragtime and jazz came into being thanks to performers like Scott Joplin. The contributions of Black blues musicians in the 1920s and 30s. Hidden figures like Daphne Oram, a BBC employee whose experiments with electronic music in the late 50s and early 70s broke new ground. And Andreas Pavel, who got to the idea of a portable music player years before Sony's Walkman.

The research for this book drew upon a million different sources: books, academic papers, museum artifacts, and speaking with professionals. Yet what we cover in this book is a just small part of the story of music and the science behind it. And, of course, music and the technology that goes with it are changing all the time. In the not-so-distant future, we'll probably be talking about applying augmented reality and virtual reality in musical settings. What comes after streaming? And we haven't even begun to talk about how musicians and songwriters will be paid for their work in the coming decades.

Music is a marvelous, mysterious and powerful thing. Learning how it all works adds new context and a whole new level of enjoyment and appreciation. We hope that this book elevates your musical experience into something even more special.

SELECTED SOURCES

Bonifield, John. "Quiz: What does your favorite music say about you?" CNN, March 31, 2016. http://www.cnn.com/2016/03/31/health/what-music-reveals-about-personality/index.html

Brown, Harriet. "How Do You Solve a Problem Like an Earworm?" *Scientific American*, November 1, 2015. http://www.scientificamerican.com/article/how-do-you-solve-a-problem-like-an-earworm/

Dawson, Victoria. "The Epic Failure of Thomas Edison's Talking Doll." *Smithsonian Magazine*, June 1, 2015. http://www.smithsonianmag.com/smithsonian-institution/epic-failure-thomas-edisons-talking-doll-180955442/

Hamilton, John. "Signing, Singing, Speaking: How Language Evolved." NPR, August 16, 2010. http://www.npr.org/templates/story/story.php?storyId=129155123

Knopper, Steve. *Appetite for Self-Destruction: The Spectacular Crash of the Record Industry in the Digital Age*. New York: Simon and Schuster, 2009.

Levitin, Daniel J. *This is Your Brain on Music*. New York: Dutton, 2006.

Lewis, Tom. *Empire of the Air: The Men Who Made Radio*. New York: Harper Perennial, 1991.

Milner, Greg. *Perfecting Sound Forever: An Aural History of Recording Music*. New York: Faber and Faber, 2009.

Owen, James. "Bone Flute Is Oldest Instrument, Study Says." *National Geographic*, June 24, 2009. http://www.nationalgeographic.com/culture/2009/06/bone-flute-is-oldest-instrument--study-says/

Taylor, Timothy D., Mark Katz and Tony Grajeda, eds. *Music, Sound, and Technology in America*. Durham, NC: Duke University Press, 2012.

Ubelacker, Sheryl. "Familiar music could give Alzheimer's patients a cognitive boost, study suggests." CBC/The Canadian Press, November 7, 2018. http://www. cbc.ca/news/health/alzheimers-music-memories-brain-scanning-1.4895791

Yong, Ed. "The Surprising Musical Preferences of an Amazon Tribe." *The Atlantic*, July 26, 2016. http://www.theatlantic.com/science/archive/2016/07/music-to-our-western-ears/491081/

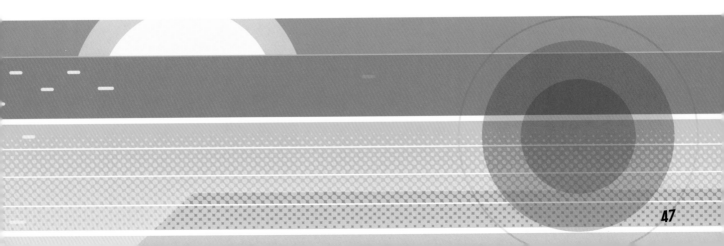

INDEX